Toby and Trish and the Amazing Book of LUKE

Published by **The Bible Reading Fellowship**
Peter's Way, Sandy Lane West
Oxford OX4 6HG
ISBN 1 84101 175 4
First edition 2000
10 9 8 7 6 5 4 3 2 1 0

Acknowledgments
Scripture quotations are taken from the Good News Bible published by The Bible Societies/HarperCollins Publishers Ltd UK © American Bible Society, 1966, 1971, 1976, 1992.
A catalogue record for this book is available from the British Library.
Printed and bound in Great Britain by Omnia Books Limited, Glasgow.

Toby and Trish
(and Boomerang!)
and the Amazing Book of

by Sue Collingbourne

Illustrated by Tom Hewitt

Welcome to the Amazing Book of LUKE!

Wanted! A scholar, writer, artist and researcher to tell a wonderful story. Luke certainly fulfilled all of these needs. Add to this a true believer and a friend of Paul, who passed Jesus' story on, and we have a wonderful, descriptive account of the life of Jesus. It's a story with pictures that cannot fail to bring us closer to Jesus.

Luke used his enquiring mind to find out every last detail. His writing, like his profession as a doctor, is the work of a careful and intelligent man. His stories were written for people just like us, and we are able to share in his great love of Jesus.

Luke lets us see Jesus as a man of the people, a man for all time.

1

Dear Theophilus

Luke 1:1–4

And so, your Excellency, because I have carefully studied all these matters from their beginning, I thought it would be good to write an orderly account for you. (Verse 3)

Have you ever been at a family party where the grown-ups begin to tell stories about each other as children? Sometimes the same event is remembered differently by the people there. As time passes, people remember different bits of the same story—usually the part that involved them most. If you took the time to write down everything they all said, then, with some careful sorting, you might find the exact version as it happened.

Luke wanted to make sure that his friend Theophilus had a really true and accurate account of the life of Jesus. He read other people's reports, he asked questions and he studied them well.

So let's look at Luke's hard work as he tells us this wonderful story.

Don't be afraid, Zechariah

Luke 1:5-13

But the angel said to him, 'Don't be afraid, Zechariah! God has heard your prayer, and your wife Elizabeth will bear you a son. You are to name him John.' (Verse 13)

Sometimes we want something so much that we ask and ask for it. It may be a new bike, a video game, the latest doll advertised on the television. Sometimes we get what we ask for, but other times we just forget about it as something new takes our fancy.

Elizabeth and Zechariah really wanted a child. They had always wanted a child. They had asked and asked God to grant this great prayer. God chose to answer them by sending the angel to Zechariah, who was a priest in the temple. But even after all those years of asking, Zechariah was taken by surprise.

Lost for words!

Luke 1:14–25

Sometimes God answers my prayers by telling me to ask for something different!

When Zechariah came out, he could not speak to them, and so they knew he had seen a vision in the Temple. Unable to say a word, he made signs to them with his hands. (Verse 22)

The angel Gabriel explained that God was going to give Elizabeth and Zechariah a wonderful gift—a son! This baby, whose name was to be John, would have a special job to do when he grew up. With the help of the Holy Spirit, he was to get everything ready for Jesus to come.

Zechariah had so many questions to ask. But he couldn't ask any of them because he was lost for words—quite literally when the angel, annoyed that Zechariah hadn't believed him, took away his speech until the baby was born.

Just as the angel had said, Elizabeth soon announced her wonderful news. She was to have the longed-for child. God had answered their prayer.

4

The chosen family
Luke 1:26-33

Boomerang doesn't have a family tree—only the one he visits every day!

Gabriel had a message for a young woman promised in marriage to a man named Joseph, who was a descendant of King David. Her name was Mary. (Verse 27)

Have you ever traced your family tree? It's a fascinating thing to do. You find out all the names of your grandparents, great-grandparents, great-great-grandparents and so on. You discover where they lived and what sort of jobs they did.

Luke did all this for Jesus. He looked back through the Old Testament and read the words of the prophets. He knew that Joseph and Mary were the people chosen to look after God's Son.

The birth of this special baby was told in a special way. The angel Gabriel came to tell Mary the news that all that had been promised was about to come true. What a surprise Mary had! We read that she was really quite upset about it all. God doesn't always make everything easy!

Mary visits Elizabeth
Luke 1:34–56

'I am the Lord's servant,' said Mary; 'may it happen to me as you have said.' And the angel left her. Soon afterwards Mary got ready and hurried off to a town in the hill country of Judea. She went into Zechariah's house and greeted Elizabeth. (Verses 38–40)

Most families have stories that they tell whenever they get together. What happened when you were born? Was there a race to the hospital? Did you arrive in the middle of the night? Who was the first person to be told?

Mary wanted to share her news with someone who would understand, and she chose Elizabeth. What a comfort this visit must have been. There was time to share news, and to prepare together for the two babies. But, above all, there was time to say 'thank you' to God.

Luke 1:1–56

Things to do

Countdown

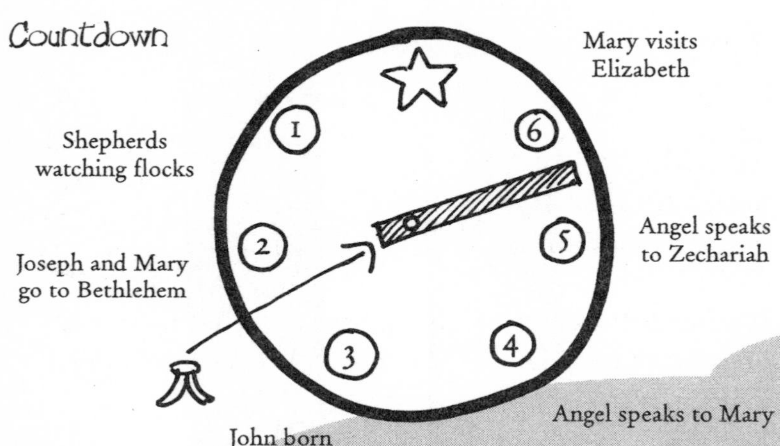

Cut out a circle from an A4 sheet of paper and a strip of card about 10 mm wide from a cereal packet. Push a split-pin paper fastener through one end of the strip of card and then through the middle of the circle to make a pointer. Which event matches which number?

6
I should have been called Patricia, but I was so small they only called me Trish

What shall we call our baby?

Luke 1:57-80

Zechariah asked for a writing tablet and wrote, 'His name is John.' How surprised they all were! (Verse 63)

When a baby is born, everyone wants to know all the details: how heavy is he; what time was he born; who does he look like; what will he be called?

It was just the same for Elizabeth and Zechariah—so many questions. The name of this new baby caused great interest. It was the custom for boy babies to take a family name, but still his name had not been announced. The neighbours turned to the silent Zechariah for an answer. With the help of a writing tablet, he said, 'His name is John'—the name given by the angel. Zechariah was rewarded by being able to speak again. He sang a song of praise. The song is full of thanks and tells of the future role of John as the one who will prepare the way for Jesus.

Baby John grew into a man and lived in the desert until the time came for his work to begin.

'Once in royal David's city...'

Luke 2:1–7

I'm glad I know exactly when I was born, so I can have birthdays

Joseph went from the town of Nazareth in Galilee to the town of Bethlehem in Judea, the birthplace of King David. Joseph went there because he was a descendant of David. (Verse 4)

Luke was a man who liked facts. He liked things to be in the right place at the right time. He had a very tidy mind! He has given us many facts in this account about Jesus' birth.

We celebrate Jesus' birthday on 25 December, but we don't really know the exact date of his birth. Early Christians chose the day because of ancient winter festivals that took place at that time of year. We know when Herod ruled and died. We know when Quirinius was governor of Syria and when Augustus was Emperor. From these dates it would seem that Jesus was born about two thousand years ago. The exact date doesn't matter, but, as Luke shows us, his birth is one of the most important events that ever happened.

What strange visitors!

Luke 2:8–20

So the shepherds hurried off and found Mary and Joseph and saw the baby lying in the manger. (Verse 16)

Most newspapers have pages in them where important announcements are published, things like the birth of a baby. Maybe your birth was announced in this way!

In a stable in Bethlehem, a very special baby was born. Luke makes us very aware of this. Jesus' arrival was not published in the local paper, it was announced by God's own messengers—the angels. The first to be told were some shepherds on the hills of Bethlehem. They were poor and uneducated—not the sort of people we might expect to be the first to hear the great news! God is full of surprises.

Thank you, Lord God, that you still send messages to us. Help us to be ready to hear and to hurry to do your will as the shepherds did. Amen

An answer to a prayer
Luke 2:21–40

'Now, Lord, you have kept your promise, and you may let your servant go in peace.' (Verse 29)

I don't remember my christening—I slept right through it

When you were a baby, you may have been baptized. If so, a sign would have been made on your forehead with water to show that you were part of God's family.

When Jesus was born, babies were not baptized. Instead Mary and Joseph took him to the temple with their 'thank you' gift to God of two doves. It was here that he was named with the name given by the angel.

Luke now tells us about Simeon and Anna. Simeon knew at once that this was the baby he had waited all of his long life to see. He was filled with such joy that, holding the baby in his arms, he sang a song of thanks to God. His song shouts out the news that Jesus is Saviour for you and me and all the world.

Jesus in the Temple
Luke 2:41–45

When Jesus was twelve years old, they went to the festival as usual. (Verse 42)

Have you ever had a great day out with your family and wished it would never end?

Luke tells us of a day like this for Jesus. He was twelve years old and had travelled to Jerusalem for the Passover festival with his family. This visit was to mark the time when Jesus would become an adult—it was his 'bar mitzvah'. Jesus was fascinated by all that he saw and heard in the Temple. He couldn't bear to leave, there was so much to learn. The women and the younger children left the city to return home and some time later the men and the older boys followed. When Joseph and Mary were together again, they realized that Jesus had not been with either of them. Like all parents would, they hurried to find their lost son.

Luke 1:57—2:45

Things to do

What's your name?	
What do your friends call you?	
What would you like to be called?	
Why?	

What's your name?

Carry out a survey among your friends to find out these 'name' facts.

Toby + Trish What's in a name?

In answer to everyone who asks why we call him Boomerang...

... he NEVER comes back!

Not the answer they expected!

Luke 2:46–52

Jesus answered them, 'Why did you have to look for me? Didn't you know that I had to be in my Father's house?' (Verse 49)

People have been finding Jesus ever since

Can you imagine how Mary and Joseph must have hurried back to Jerusalem? Can you imagine them searching all the places they had visited, asking everyone they met if they had seen Jesus?

Finally Mary and Joseph returned to the temple grounds. They were crowded with people wanting to hear the important speakers and teachers. Maybe, just maybe, Jesus would be here. And then they saw him sitting among the teachers, listening and asking them questions. Like all mothers, in her relief at finding him safe, Mary became cross with Jesus. She said, 'Your father and I have been terribly worried trying to find you'.

Luke has recorded for us the first words of Jesus to be written down, and what words they are! Jesus tells Mary and Joseph that he has realized who he is. He knows he is the Son of God.

A man from the desert

Luke 3:1-16

'Someone is shouting in the desert: "Get the road ready for the Lord; make a straight path for him to travel!"' (Verse 4)

Once again we hear of John, the son of Elizabeth. He is a man now and he has spent many years praying and teaching about the time when God's Son would arrive—the person he knew as Jesus.

Someone I once knew owned a small clay pot, nothing much to look at and not really of any great value. But this small pot was probably one of the most important things she owned. It was just the right size to hold open her kitchen window without it banging shut in a breeze! Its value was indeed beyond measure. Jesus was a bit like that pot. Easily overlooked by many, it took just one person to recognize his real worth.

John was that person.

13
I can put my head under the water if I hold my nose

Jesus is baptized

Luke 3:16–22

'I baptize you with water, but someone is coming who is much greater than I am. I am not good enough even to untie his sandals. He will baptize you with the Holy Spirit and fire.' *(Verse 16)*

When John baptized people and told them that God had forgiven them all the things they had done wrong, they began to wonder if he was the one they had been waiting for.

John could have let people go on believing that he was someone he was not, but he decided to put the record straight. He told the crowd in no uncertain terms that they were mistaken—he was not the Son of God.

The moment John had waited for came. Jesus stepped quietly forward and walked into the water to be baptized by John. The beginning of Jesus' work is marked in this way—with the gift of the Holy Spirit and a voice from heaven telling everyone that Jesus was the Son of God.

14

The ancestors
Luke 3:23-38

When Jesus began his work, he was about 30 years old. He was the son, so people thought, of Joseph, who was the son of Heli. (Verse 23)

There's a song that goes, 'There was an old lady who swallowed a fly, I don't know why she swallowed a fly, perhaps she'll die. There was an old lady who swallowed a spider, that wriggled and wriggled and tickled inside her. She swallowed the spider to catch the fly, I don't know why she swallowed the fly...' and so on. The whole idea of the song is to remember the things she swallowed in the right order without making any mistakes.

In Jesus' day, a person's family line was like this. People could recite it from memory. The family line was so important that Luke has given us Jesus' family line. He has written it down to mark the time when Jesus began his work. The family line shows us who Jesus was, back through the generations until the time of Adam.

Time to think
Luke 4:1-13

But Jesus answered, 'The scripture says, "Do not put the Lord your God to the test."' (Verse 12)

These adverts on telly tempt me all the time

Jesus had decided to start his important work, but first of all he needed time on his own just to think.

Luke tells us that the devil came to try to spoil it all. Jesus was in a lonely place without any food. How easy it would have been to have given in and gone home. Perhaps you have promised to do a small task for your mum and your friends come round to play. Do you do the task first or do you forget about it and go out? We call this being 'tempted'. Jesus didn't forget his task, even when it became really hard to say 'no' to the devil.

What sometimes tempts you? Things to make you comfortable, things to make you look important, or things to make you the leader of the gang? Jesus said 'no' to all these things.

Luke 2:45—4:13

Things to do

A great team

Colour in this picture of the amazing moment when God the Father, God the Son and God the Holy Spirit were all there by the River Jordan.

Toby + Trish Not team material

I enjoyed playing footers with you, bro
Yes, it's certainly a faster-moving game with TWO balls!

16

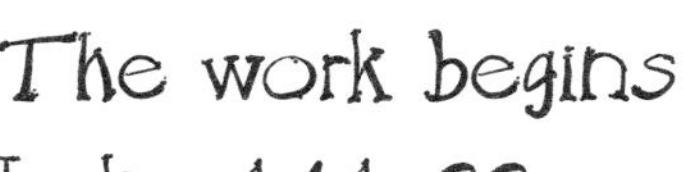

The work begins
Luke 4:14–22

Jesus taught in the synagogues and was praised by everyone. (Verse 15)

At last the work had begun. Jesus left the desert and went back home to Galilee. He was soon being talked about in all the villages. People began to listen to what he had to say. Jesus went to the synagogue in Nazareth on the Saturday, the Sabbath. It was here that he had been taught the scriptures as a child. He knew the place and the scriptures well.

Hundreds of years before Jesus was born, the prophet Isaiah spoke of a special man who God would choose to help those who were poor, or prisoners of war, or blind or being bullied. Jesus read Isaiah's words aloud that day and when he had finished he rolled up the scroll and told everyone that the words had come true. Jesus was God's Chosen One, the Messiah.

Can you imagine how people must have felt? They had known him from his childhood. They were impressed by what they had heard—but would it last?

The crowd turns nasty

Luke 4:23–30

The people meant to throw Jesus over the cliff, but he walked through the middle of the crowd and went his way. (Verses 29–30)

...and now millions of tourists go to Nazareth to see where Jesus lived

Sometimes a new pop group is followed everywhere. The newspapers photograph them and write all sorts of things about how they dress and what places they visit in their spare time. The magazines are full of the tiniest details about their lives. They become idols. Then something is written about them that is not so good. The fans stop buying the CDs and no one bothers to follow them any more.

At first, people in the synagogue were impressed by what Jesus said. But as he went on, they became really angry. Jesus told them that everyone was important to God, no matter what their religion or race. The people didn't want to hear this and they took Jesus to the cliff-top to kill him. Somehow he managed to escape the crowd, and he left Nazareth, never to return.

Many people are healed

Luke 4:31-44

After sunset all who had friends who were sick with various diseases brought them to Jesus; he placed his hands on every one of them and healed them all. *(Verse 40)*

Immediately after leaving Nazareth, Jesus went to Capernaum, a city on the lakeside. He amazed everyone in the synagogue with his teaching. Among those present was a man who had been ill for many years with a troubled mind. Ill as he was, this man knew that Jesus was someone who could help him. He knew that Jesus had been sent by God. The man called out for help. Jesus ordered the evil thoughts to leave the man alone, and they did! That evening Jesus went to rest at the home of his friend, Simon, but even here he was asked to use his powers and make Simon's mother-in-law well.

It was no wonder that news spread about Jesus. People began to bring those who were unwell to him. They began to ask, 'Is this the Son of God?'

19

A favourite place
Luke 5:1–3

Jesus saw two boats pulled up on the beach; the fishermen had left them and were washing the nets. (Verse 2)

Do you have a favourite place that you and your friends have made your own?

Sometimes favourite places have many different names. In our country, towns can be known by the old Roman name, a local name and the name to be found on a modern map. Lake Galilee was just such a place. It was also known as the Sea of Tiberias or, as Luke has written, the Lake of Gennesaret. When Jesus walked along its shores, there were nine towns clustered around it. It was a busy place, full of people working and travelling, and Jesus would have known many people there. It was one of his favourite places.

His friend Simon lived in one of the towns and fished on the lake. So many people wanted to hear Jesus speak that the synagogue was not big enough any more, so he began to teach in the open air. Luke tells us about the day that Jesus used Simon's boat out on the water to speak to the crowd.

20

I'm not going to catch anything. I wonder if Jesus would still want me...?

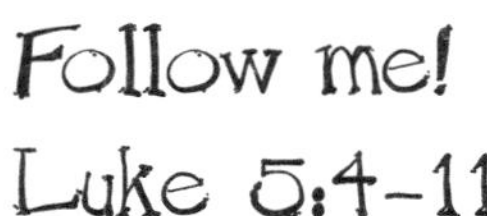

Follow me!
Luke 5:4–11

The fishermen pulled the boats up on the beach, left everything, and followed Jesus. (Verse 11)

'Push the boat out further,' said Jesus to Simon. Even though they had fished all night, Simon did as Jesus said. He was rewarded with a huge catch of fish, so big that he needed help from other boats to pull the heavy nets back in.

Of course, Simon wanted to thank Jesus. He was so amazed at what Jesus had done that he realized just how great Jesus was. Jesus knew that Simon, James and John were just the sort of friends he needed—friends to help him with his special work. When Jesus asked them to go with him, they did not hesitate to leave their boats and become 'fishers of people'.

The fish became a secret sign for the early Christians. It meant that Jesus was with them. The Greek word for fish is *ichthus*. The word and the symbol were used as a secret code in the days when it was dangerous to be a Christian.

Luke 4:14—5:11

Things to do

Secret sign

Using candle wax, draw this fish sign on a sheet of A4 paper. Using water-colours, paint a picture over it of Lake Galilee, with a blue sky, blue water and lots of fishing boats. Your secret sign will appear in the picture.

Toby + Trish Not so secret

... and this is a secret sign to show my pocket money's spent...

21

Faith can heal!
Luke 5:12-25

Once Jesus was in a town where there was a man who was suffering from a dreaded skin disease. When he saw Jesus, he threw himself down and begged him, 'Sir, if you want to, you can make me clean!' (Verse 12)

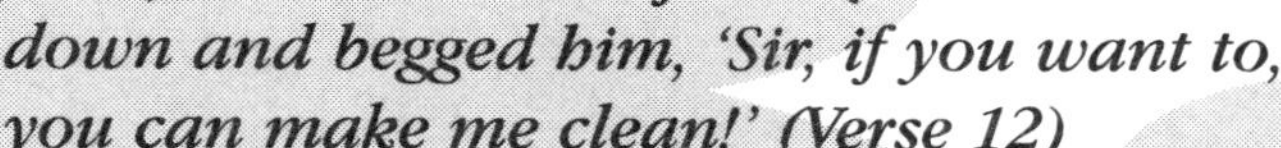

'Unclean! Unclean!' would have been a common cry in Galilee in Jesus' day. One of the most feared diseases was leprosy. People suffering from the disease were not allowed near other people and they had to shout out to let everyone know they were near. One man called out to be healed. Jesus did what no one else would do: he touched him. Because the man had believed in Jesus, he was made well.

Word spread quickly and more and more people who were unwell were brought to Jesus. Luke tells us about a man who was lowered through the roof for Jesus to touch. But not everyone was pleased with what they saw and heard. Some Jewish teachers of the law and religious leaders (Pharisees) were very angry. Jesus had made some enemies.

Levi Joins Jesus
Luke 5:27-31

Levi got up, left everything, and followed Jesus.
(Verse 28)

In Jesus' day, tax collectors were not liked at all and they lived life away from the townspeople. Levi was a wealthy man—he worked for the Roman government. The tax booths were outside the city gates, and it was here that Jesus saw Levi, who is also known as Matthew.

Levi did not hesitate when Jesus said, 'Follow me.' He must have known that he could never return to his job—the Romans would not have taken him back.

Levi was so pleased to have been chosen by Jesus that he gave a great party to celebrate—he wanted everyone to know! Some Pharisees, the enemies of Jesus, came to complain because Jesus was being friendly with a hated tax collector. Jesus told them that he had come for people who needed his help, not for those who did not.

Questions!

Luke 5:33—6:11

Some Pharisees asked, 'Why are you doing what our Law says you cannot do on the Sabbath?' (Verse 2)

The disciples were happy to be with Jesus, and it showed! The religious men of the day couldn't understand this. To them, worshipping God was a serious business—no time to think of being happy.

One of their rules was to go without food at certain times in order to concentrate on God. But the disciples didn't always follow the rules. The Pharisees tried to trick Jesus into saying the rules were wrong, but he was much too clever for them. They tried again when they saw the disciples picking corn to eat. The Pharisees said that no one must work on the Sabbath. Once again, Jesus was too clever for them. Jesus even healed a man with a paralysed hand on the Sabbath. More enemies were made.

24

Twelve men to choose
Luke 6:12-16

When day came, Jesus called his disciples to him and chose twelve of them, whom he named apostles. (Verse13)

So many enemies! Jesus needed people he could trust to carry on the work after he was gone. Luke tells us that Jesus prayed and then called all of his friends to him.

A long time ago, Moses led twelve tribes of Israel to the land promised them by God, and now Jesus chooses twelve men to be his apostles. The word 'apostle' means 'someone sent' or a messenger. They were to send the message of Jesus all over the world.

We have already met Simon, James, John and Levi. To join these four, Jesus chose Andrew the brother of Simon, Simon the Zealot, Philip, Thomas, Bartholomew, James, Judas and Judas Iscariot. They were a real mixture—fishermen, a tax collector, a money keeper and a hot-head who wanted to fight the Romans! They were ordinary people who would take on an extraordinary job.

Happiness is...

Luke 6:17–26

Jesus looked at his disciples and said, 'Happy are you poor; the Kingdom of God is yours!' (Verse 20)

After the apostles had been chosen, Jesus went with them down the hillside where there were many people waiting for him. Many had come to hear him speak and to be healed. Jesus surprised them all with what he had to say.

There is an old song that goes something like this: 'Happiness, happiness, the greatest gift that I possess.' I wonder what makes you happy. The people Jesus called 'happy' are just the ones we might expect to be the most miserable. But Jesus knew that real happiness is not found easily. People who find life to be very difficult will be happy in God's kingdom because they will have more than money could buy.

Dear Lord, help me to understand that happiness is nothing to do with having lots of things—it is to do with the sort of person I really am. Amen

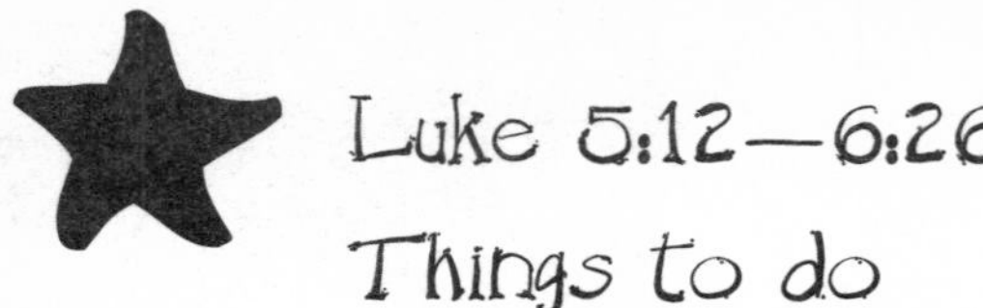

Luke 5:12—6:26

Things to do

The secret of...

To discover the secret, find a word that goes all the way down the middle of the puzzle!

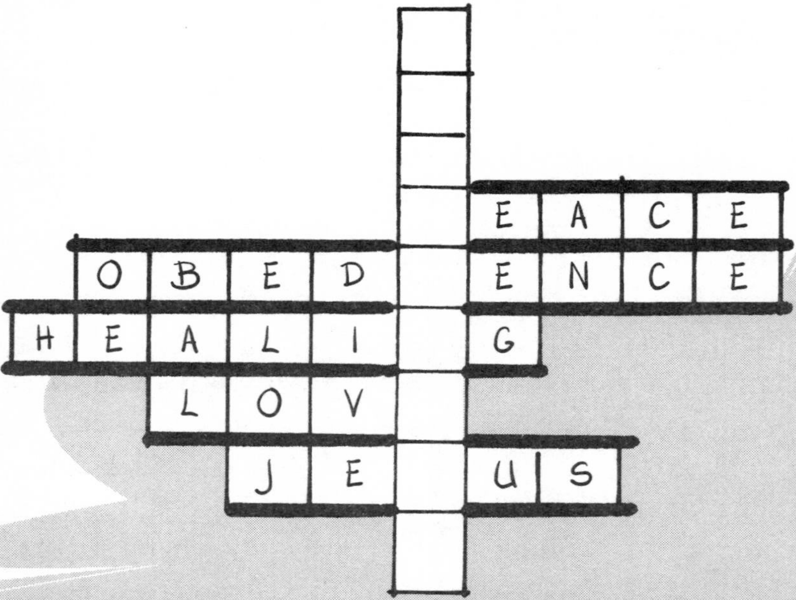

_ E A C E
O B E D _ E N C E
H E A L I _ G
L O V _
J E _ U S

Toby + Trish

Wrong sums

I've figured out the secret of how to make your pocket money last for ever...

Spend your sister's!

Love your enemies
Luke 6:27–36

'Do for others just what you want them to do for you.' (Verse 31)

I wonder what you would do if someone threatened to hit you? Would you threaten them back? What would you do if someone talked about you behind your back? Would you talk about them? Be really honest with your answers! Jesus said that even when someone is being really horrid, we must not be horrid back!

There are all sorts of rules—school rules, road rules, countryside rules, family rules. But Jesus gave a special rule called 'The Golden Rule': 'Treat others just as you want them to treat you!'

Good and bad in all of us

Luke 6:37–42

They complain about feeding me once a day—and *they're* eating all day long!

'Do not judge others, and God will not judge you; do not condemn others, and God will not condemn you; forgive others, and God will forgive you.' (Verse 37)

Have you ever criticized a friend for not doing something they said they would do? Did you bother to find out why they hadn't done it? And when they asked you about your reason for not doing something you said you would do, did you think you had a good excuse?

We call this having a double standard. It's just not fair to expect things of other people that we are not willing to expect of ourselves. Jesus told a funny story of a man with a plank in his eye who was busy trying to take a speck out of his brother's eye. The man could not see his own faults, only the smaller faults of his brother.

Trees, people and houses!
Luke 6:43-49

***'A healthy tree does not bear bad fruit, nor does a poor tree bear good fruit.'* (Verse 43)**

Sometimes it is far better to say something by painting a picture than by writing it down. Jesus often 'painted pictures' with words. He told stories of everyday things that we can easily imagine, but those everyday things have a very special meaning. It is easy to see the trees he spoke about, and it is easy to understand that healthy apple trees give good apples. It's just the same with people. People with good thoughts will do good things for others, and people with nasty thoughts will do nasty things.

We all know it is silly to build a house on sand, because it will be washed away when the tide comes in. Jesus knew that people are just the same. If our life is not lived by Jesus' rules, very soon things will begin to go wrong.

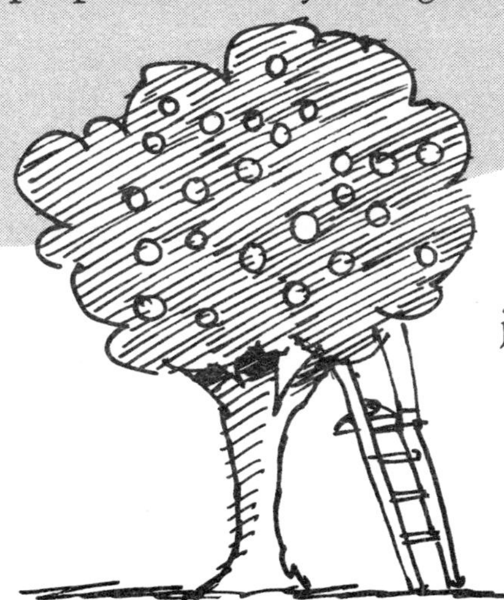

More miracles
Luke 7:1–17

This news about Jesus went out through all the country and the surrounding territory. (Verse 17)

If I pass this test, it will be a miracle!

In Jesus' day, everyone believed in miracles. They all knew about the miracles written in the Old Testament. They all knew about the 'miracle workers' who travelled the towns. The miracles that Jesus made happen were very important to Luke and the other Gospel writers. They tell us of about thirty-five different miracles.

Jesus used his power from God at Capernaum to heal a Roman officer's servant and he used the power again in Nain to bring a widow's son back to life. Jesus didn't make miracles happen for effect. He wanted to show people how to trust God at all times and how much God cared for them.

Say what you see!
Luke 7:18-35

I know this much—I passed the test!

'John is greater than anyone who has ever lived. But the one who is least in the Kingdom of God is greater than John.' (Verse 28)

John had heard all about Jesus—he had known him from childhood. He knew all the things he had been saying and doing. But when he was in prison John still sent some of his friends to find out more! Jesus sent them away. 'Go back and tell him what you have seen and heard,' he said.

We too know the things that Jesus had been saying and doing—Luke tells us all about them. Jesus knew that John was special because his job was to prepare the way for Jesus, but John would never know about Jesus dying on the cross and rising to life again.

Jesus says that we are greater than John because we know the rest of Jesus' amazing story.

Dear Jesus, thank you that you died and rose again for me. Help me to find out as much as I can about you and then to tell others. Amen

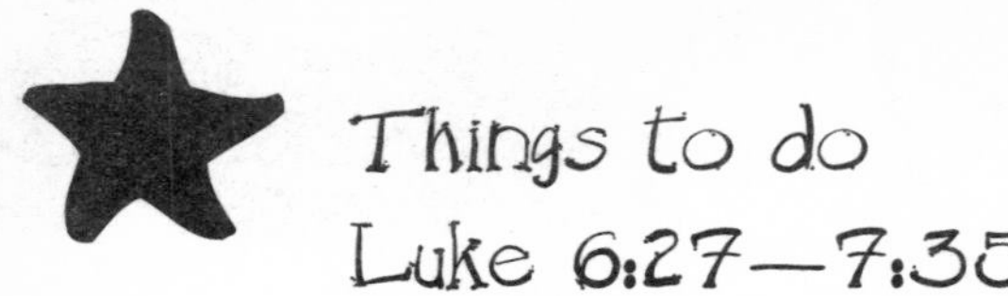

Things to do
Luke 6:27—7:35

Telegram to John

A few years ago, the only way to get an urgent message to somebody without a telephone was to send a telegram. Imagine you have only 15 words to tell John what is happening…

Toby + Trish Short and sweet

I got a postcard from the seaside—it's only got three words on it…

'Great time! Kylie'

At the Pharisee's house
Luke 7:36-50

'You did not welcome me with a kiss, but she has not stopped kissing my feet since I came. You provided no olive oil for my head, but she has covered my feet with perfume.' (Verses 45 and 46)

When a guest comes to your house, I expect that someone takes their coat, shows them where to sit down and offers them a nice cup of tea!

It was just the same in Jesus' time. The guest was treated as a very special person. When a guest came, three things were done. A kiss of welcome was placed on their cheek, a bowl of water was offered to wash the dust from their feet, and a drop of sweet-smelling oil was placed on their head as a sign of friendship. Luke tells us that Simon the Pharisee forgot all of these things when Jesus came to his house. It was left to an outsider to do. She washed his feet with her tears and dried them with her hair. She kissed his feet and covered them in perfume. Jesus told them that such love would be rewarded.

32

Jesus on tour

Luke 8:1-3

Some time later Jesus travelled through towns and villages, preaching the Good News about the Kingdom of God. The twelve disciples went with him, and so did some women who had been healed. (Verses 1 and 2)

Jesus had made many enemies as he travelled around Galilee. He didn't always say what the religious leaders wanted to hear—Jesus had a different message to tell. One by one, the synagogues were closed to him and he had to teach in the open air or in people's homes. He travelled from town to town, teaching and eating and sleeping wherever he was welcome.

But he didn't travel alone. The twelve chosen friends went with him and also some women whom he had healed. The rabbis did not teach women, but Jesus welcomed them in his travelling group. Luke tells us about Mary Magdalene, Joanna and Susanna who gave money to buy food for Jesus and the others. What a mixed group they were!

The sower and the seed
Luke 8:4-15

'And some seeds fell in good soil; the plants grew and produced corn, a hundred grains each.' And Jesus concluded, 'Listen, then, if you have ears!' (Verse 8)

Jesus taught in parables. Parables are stories about things we see every day and understand well, but they have a special message within them from God.

Jesus used parables to teach people about God. The parable of the sower did this. His listeners would have seen a sower at work many times. They knew the land well—it had many rocky and shallow places. They would have seen the birds swooping down for a good feed. But this wasn't just a story. There was a message as well! The seeds are the word of God, and it is up to the listeners to decide which type of soil they are and which they want to become. Jesus wants us all to be good ground, ready to take God's word and let it grow.

Something I heard last Sunday keeps going round in my head

I wish your recorder could be hidden away and covered up!

34

Things hidden away
Luke 8:16–18

***'Whatever is hidden away will be brought out into the open, and whatever is covered up will be found and brought to light.'* (Verse 17)**

Imagine that you have to put on your best clothes to go and visit a relative. Just as you are about to leave, some friends knock at the door and make fun of how you are dressed—you look very different. Jesus tells us that people who believe in him are often laughed at and made to feel different, but we must not stop believing just because of this.

If you have ever learnt to play a musical instrument, you will know that you need to practise a lot! If you give up because it's too hard and takes too much time, you'll no longer be able to play. Being a Christian is a bit the same—it needs lots of practice! If we don't practise, we might forget how!

Help me to show others that I believe in you, Lord Jesus. When things seem hard, thank you for showing me that it's worth getting right. Amen

Jesus' mother and brothers
Luke 8:19–21

Jesus' mother and brothers came to him, but were unable to join him because of the crowd. Someone said to Jesus, 'Your mother and brothers are standing outside and want to see you.' (Verses 19 and 20)

Many thousands of artists have painted pictures or sculpted statues of how Jesus may have looked. Often the artists show him as a baby being nursed by Mary, his mother. Other artists have shown him as a man. Sometimes the grown-up Jesus is shown with Mary.

There is a very beautiful statue in St Peter's, Rome, of Mary holding the limp body of Jesus. It is called 'The *Pieta*', which means 'Pity'. There is no doubt that Jesus loved his mother and the rest of his family very much.

Luke tells us that Mary and Jesus' brothers came to see him, but Jesus knew that now his work had begun, he no longer belonged just to them. Jesus tells us that all people everywhere are a part of his family, too.

Luke 7:36—8:21

Things to do

Jesus' family

Families usually look alike, but not God's family! People of every race, size, age and shape belong to it. Draw and cut out some finger puppets from thick paper or card of all the different people.

Toby + Trish Unemployed

If Boomerang is one of the family, why doesn't he DO anything...?
I don't like it when he starts thinking!

36

The great thing about the swimming-pool is that you know when the next wave's coming

A frightening boat ride

Luke 8:22–23

***As they were sailing, Jesus fell asleep. Suddenly a strong wind blew down on the lake, and the boat began to fill with water, so that they were all in great danger.* (Verse 23)**

'It's like being in a wind tunnel,' someone was heard to say in the local shopping mall. Whenever the wind blows, people clutch on to their clothes and shopping!

Lake Galilee is in a sort of wind tunnel. It is low down with hills each side, and when the wind blows the water soon becomes very choppy. Crossing the lake in a boat is the easiest way to get to the towns on either side of the shore, and Luke tells us about one of these journeys.

It started in an ordinary way, with Jesus and his friends doing something they had done many times before—so ordinary that Jesus fell asleep. The tunnel filled with a wind and the water changed from gentle and calm to stormy and very frightening.

The disciples didn't know what to do!

37
I wonder if Mum can help me keep this hat on in the wind!

Who is this man?

Luke 8:24-25

Then Jesus said to the disciples, 'Where is your faith?' But they were amazed and afraid, and said to one another, 'Who is this man? He gives orders to the winds and waves, and they obey him!' (Verse 25)

Who do you ask for help when you are in trouble? One of your parents, your teacher, a friend? Or do you speak with God in a prayer?

The disciples went straight to Jesus and told him they were all going to drown. Luke tells us that Jesus calmed the wind and the lake was safe again.

How sad he must have been. Even his closest friends had not really believed that he would be able to help them.

Are you, like the disciples, beginning to realize that Jesus was no ordinary person?

A man called Mob

Luke 8:26–31

That man had no one to help him but Jesus

As Jesus stepped ashore, he was met by a man from the town who had demons in him. For a long time this man had gone without clothes and would not stay at home, but spent his time in the burial caves. (Verse 27)

Jesus had calmed the storm. The boat travelled on to Gerasa, a town on the other side of the lake. He was met by a poor man who was not in his right mind. In those days such an illness would have been blamed on 'demons'.

It seems strange that the disciples had not been sure about Jesus' power when they were on the lake, but that this poor man knew exactly who Jesus was! Without knowing it, he even answered the question the disciples had asked just a short while before—'Who is this man?'—when he cried out loud, 'Jesus, Son of the Most High God!'

39

A herd of pigs
Luke 8:32-39

The demons went out of the man and into the pigs. The whole herd rushed down the side of the cliff into the lake and was drowned. (Verse 33)

In those days, because people believed that illness was caused by 'demons', they also believed that you were cured when the demons left. So Jesus calls the demons to come out of the man.

The problem of stopping them from coming back was solved when the herd of pigs and the demons drowned together and the poor man could at last think clearly.

He wanted to get into the boat with Jesus and follow him, but Jesus knew that the man had a job to do in his own town—a job of telling the others about what had happened. When Jesus does something for us, we need to tell others about it, too!

The end of a busy day!

Luke 8:40–42, 49–56

A messenger came from the official's house. 'Your daughter has died,' he told Jairus; 'don't bother the Teacher any longer.' But Jesus heard it and said to Jairus, 'Don't be afraid; only believe, and she will be well.' (Verses 49 and 50)

I wonder what you would think makes a busy day? Maybe you get up early, catch the bus to school and spend the day in lessons. When you get home, it's tea-time, homework, television, Cubs, Brownies, judo, swimming or some other activity with your friends, supper and off to bed! All pretty exhausting, but fun all the same.

Jesus had already calmed a storm, tried to explain to his friends who he was, and cured a man who desperately needed help, and the day wasn't over yet. On the other side of the lake, more people waited who needed his help. Jairus had waited because his daughter was dying—Jesus was his last hope. When told it was too late, Jesus hurried to the house and, tired as he was, he did what had seemed impossible. The little girl sat up and even ate a good meal.

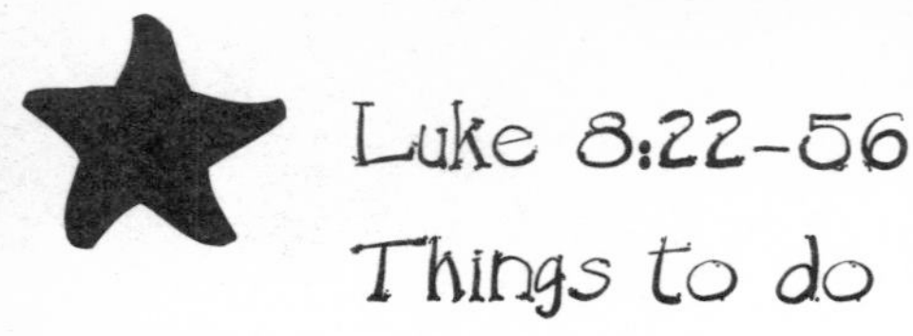

Luke 8:22-56

Things to do

A day in the life of...

Make a television camera out of a cereal packet and a card tube. With your friends or family, film a short newsreel of a day in the life of Jesus.

Toby + Trish The long view

It's been a long day—
I've watched 36 television programmes! Hope I'm well enough to go to school tomorrow

The woman who touched Jesus
Luke 8:43-48

The woman came up in the crowd behind Jesus and touched the edge of his cloak, and her bleeding stopped at once. Jesus asked, 'Who touched me?' (Verses 44 and 45)

Imagine you are all ready to leave the house. You are a bit late, but there is just enough time to get to the airport to catch the plane for holidays. Then, disaster, the phone rings! 'Leave it, Mum,' you cry. But your mum stops and picks up the receiver. Will you be in time for that flight?

Jesus was on his way to Jairus' house when something made him stop. A woman had reached out of the crowd and touched him. She believed that by doing this she would be made well. He was so impressed by her faith in him that he used precious moments to speak to her.

42

The disciples have work to do

Luke 9:1-6

Then Jesus sent the disciples out to preach the Kingdom of God and to heal the sick. (Verse 2)

If there had been a newspaper called *The Galilee Times* it might have printed a job advertisement that said, 'Freelance healers wanted! We are looking for suitable candidates for an important new project working with the homeless in Galilee. The ability to work alone for little money is essential. Are you intrigued? Interested? Apply straight away!'

Jesus had taken his disciples everywhere with him. They had listened and watched him at work. It was now time to send them out to use the powers he had given them. They were told to go and teach people about God and then come back and tell him what they had done. 'Travel light' was their instruction. Possessions are not important to do the work of Jesus.

I throw the ball, Boomerang.
You fetch it!

Herod is a worried man
Luke 9:7–9

When Herod, the ruler of Galilee,

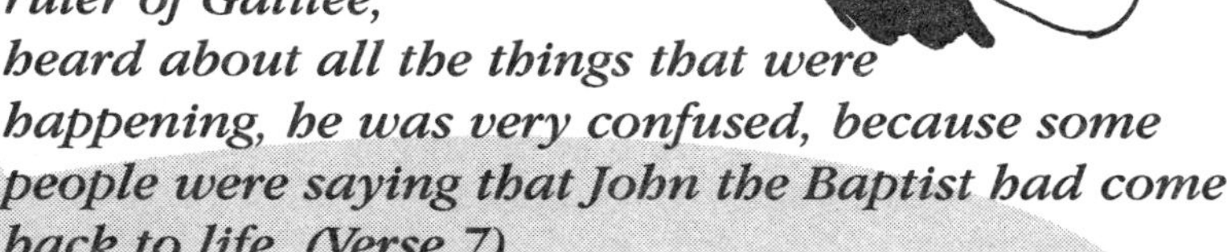

heard about all the things that were happening, he was very confused, because some people were saying that John the Baptist had come back to life. (Verse 7)

Throughout the ages, people have pictured Jesus in many different ways. Some have seen him as a wonderful teacher, others as a great healer. Some have seen straight away that he is God's Son. The songs and hymns we sing often describe how people see him. In one we sing of 'Gentle Jesus, meek and mild', in another 'Jesus is Lord of all'. How would you describe Jesus?

Herod knew exactly what he thought of Jesus—he was a nuisance and someone to be feared. Herod was afraid that this new king would come and take away all of his wealth and power. And now there were more nuisances! The disciples were busy doing the work Jesus had sent them to do. Herod had got rid of John, but how was he to get rid of Jesus and his disciples?

It's good to be back!

Luke 9:10–11

It's been such a long holiday, I can't remember where the school is

When the crowds heard about it, they followed him. He welcomed them, spoke to them about the Kingdom of God, and healed those who needed it. (Verse 11)

When the school holidays begin, everyone is very happy. The thought of all the days to enjoy, places to visit and things to do is very exciting. But a strange thing happens as the holiday goes on. Time seems to go very slowly. We begin to get bored and miss our friends. It is good to go back at the beginning of a new term and share our holiday adventures.

The disciples had been away from Jesus, working on their own. How good it must have been to be back with him. There was so much to talk about! They travelled to the town of Bethsaida to be together, but it wasn't long before the people found out where they were. The news had to wait—there was work to do.

45
Boomerang takes a few dog biscuits when we have a picnic

Five thousand hungry people
Luke 9:12–17

Jesus took the five loaves and two fish, looked up to heaven, thanked God for them, broke them, and gave them to the disciples to distribute to the people. (Verse 16)

Try to imagine sitting outside on a hillside in the hot sun for many hours. You have nothing with you to eat or drink, and yet the time seems to pass very quickly because you are really interested in what you are doing.

Luke now shares with us one of the most wonderful stories we may ever read. It was so wonderful that Matthew, Mark and John also tell us about it in their amazing books. Five thousand people had sat all day listening to Jesus. The disciples wanted to send them home to eat and rest. Jesus told them to stay, and used the food that was provided—five loaves and two fish—to feed them all. It was a great miracle. Once again, Jesus provided everything that the people needed.

Luke 8:43—9:17

Things to do

Impossible?

Take a strip of paper. Twist it once before taping the ends together. Then ask your friends and family how many sides a piece of paper has. When they say 'two', ask them to take a pencil and draw along one side of the paper until the line joins up. The impossible has happened!

Toby + Trish
Can't be done
Give me a sum to try on my new calculator
Two minus ten
You're just trying to bust it!

46

Who am I?

Luke 9:18-20

One day when Jesus was praying alone, the disciples came to him. 'Who do the crowds say I am?' he asked them. (Verse 18)

Many people keep a diary. Do you have one? What sort of things do you write in it? Whatever you write, a diary contains a record of events that are important to you.

Luke has written about one of the most important events at this time of Jesus' life. The disciples had been with him for almost three years. They had learnt such a lot! Jesus had to be sure that they understood who he was and what they had to do when he was gone from them. What a wonderful day this must have been for Jesus. At last Peter really understood! 'Who do you say I am?' Jesus asked. Peter answered, 'You are God's Messiah'.

Dear God, thank you that your very own Son came to show us what you are like. Amen

A secret to keep

Luke 9:21–27

So that's why you hid my slipper in your basket—you've chewed a hole in it

Then Jesus gave them strict orders not to tell this to anyone. (Verse 21)

A small girl, about five years old, had a very large white rabbit as a pet. She looked after it very well. It was fed only the best food, the cage was cleaned every day, and she loved it very much. One day, when she was in school, the rabbit died. Her parents didn't know how they would tell her the awful news. They decided to go to the pet shop and buy another rabbit the same as the one that had died. When the girl came home, she knew straight away that this rabbit was not hers. She wanted to know the truth.

The time had come to explain to the disciples what Jesus already knew about his future—to give them the truth. He told them that one day soon he would have to leave them to die on a cross, but that this wasn't the end—he would be given life again after three days. The disciples had to keep this secret for a while. The time to share would come much later.

Inside a shining light

Luke 9:28–36

Jesus took Peter, John, and James with him and went up a hill to pray. While he was praying, his face changed its appearance, and his clothes became dazzling white. (Verses 28 and 29)

When a famous football player or a famous pop star comes into town, everyone recognizes them. When Jesus travelled through the towns of Galilee, everyone recognized him. His twelve special friends would have known him anywhere.

But Jesus could still surprise them! Peter, James and John were allowed to see not only the Jesus they saw every day, but also the Jesus that God recognized. Jesus' face and clothes changed and the three disciples became confused, until they heard God's voice telling them that Jesus was his Son. They decided to keep this secret to themselves.

A boy to be healed

Luke 9:37–43

Mum says you've got to come down and help with tea

The next day, Jesus and the three disciples went down from the hill, and a large crowd met Jesus. A man shouted from the crowd, 'Teacher! I beg you, look at my son—my only son!' (Verses 37 and 38)

Birthday parties are a wonderful time: friends to play with, cards and presents to open, being the centre of attention. Sometimes we just don't want it all to end. Everything is very exciting and busy.

Peter felt a bit like that on the mountain. He had seen and heard wonderful things. He didn't want to leave. But Jesus took them with him, to where still more crowds waited. A man shouted from the crowd for Jesus to heal his son. He had already asked the other disciples to help, but they couldn't make the boy well. Jesus was really disappointed that they had not believed enough in the power he had given them, but this did not stop him from helping the boy. I wonder—if you were really disappointed, would you be able to put it all to one side and still think of others?

50
We mustn't forget we're washing up

Remember this!
Luke 9:34–45

The people were still marvelling at everything Jesus was doing, when he said to his disciples, 'Don't forget what I am about to tell you! The Son of Man is going to be handed over to the power of human beings.' (Verses 43 and 44)

Can you imagine a football crowd or the audience at a pop concert? There is excitement everywhere—people are rushing around trying to find their seats and to buy food and souvenirs. For a little while, they may even have forgotten why they have come—all the activities have taken over their whole attention. It takes a voice on the loudspeaker to draw them back to the event and tell them to take their seats so that the game or the show can begin.

Jesus faced a situation like this. The crowds and the disciples were so excited by the things he was doing that they had forgotten why he had come. Jesus took just a moment to bring them down to earth. But still they did not really understand.

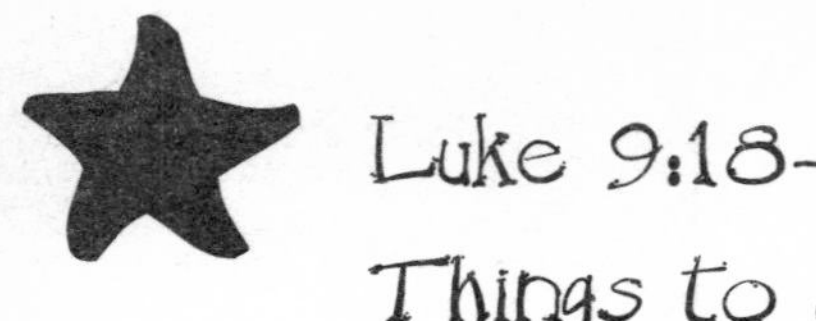

Luke 9:18-45

Things to do

Light and shadow

Next to the words that God spoke, trace over the picture of Jesus in the light.

Around the words that Jesus said to his disciples, draw a thick, black shadow.

This is my Son,
whom I have chosen'

'The Son of Man is going to be
handed over to the power of
human beings'

Toby + Trish Light and shade

It's fine under this sunshade— but my legs are going to look as if they belong to someone else!

Who is the greatest?

Luke 9:46-50

An argument broke out among the disciples as to which one of them was the greatest. (Verse 46)

A man called Muhammed Ali once made his living as a boxer. Everywhere he went, he boasted that he was the greatest! He won many fights until the day came when he was beaten. He could no longer use that boast. People boast about all sorts of things to try and seem important, or to try to impress someone else. Do you know anyone like that?

The disciples had failed in healing the little boy and now they wanted to be important in front of Jesus. They were jealous of each other. Jesus knew exactly what they were thinking and he chose a child to sit next to him. Jesus wanted the disciples to understand that the most important thing of all was to help one another and other people. Each one of his disciples had important work to do.

A village in Samaria

Luke 9:51-56

Jesus made up his mind and set out on his way to Jerusalem. He sent messengers ahead of him, who went into a village in Samaria to get everything ready for him. (Verses 51 and 52)

Have you ever heard of the expression, 'Like a red rag to a bull'? It refers to the idea that bulls become very angry if they see anything red and try to chase it away.

Here Luke tells us of a 'red rag' incident. Jesus knew that the time had come to make his last journey to Jerusalem. There were several roads he could have chosen, but he took the disciples through Samaria. For many years, the Jewish people and the Samaritan people had quarrelled with each other. Jesus knew this, but he still went that way. The people were very unfriendly to the travellers and the disciples wanted to teach them a lesson. Jesus would not hear of it. He wanted the disciples to be friendly even to their enemies. Would you do the same?

Lots of excuses
Luke 9:57–62

It's funny how
I never quite
get round to
tidying my
bedroom

As they went on their way, a man said to Jesus, 'I will follow you wherever you go.' (Verse 57)

There is an old Russian story about a woman called Baboushka. She really wanted to go and see the Christ-child, but she also wanted to tidy up at home first. The story tells us that when she eventually left to find the baby Jesus, it was too late. Everywhere she looked, the family had been there but had just left. The story says that she never found the baby and is still searching.

Jesus knows that sometimes we don't have lots of time, but we must go with him straight away. If, like Baboushka, we keep putting it off, then it might all be too late. There is an old saying that goes, 'Don't put off till tomorrow what you can do today!'

Lord Jesus, help me to do what I need to do today and not put things off until it is too late. Amen

Seventy-two helpers
Luke 10:1-24

His helpers went out two by two, hurray, hurray...

The Lord chose another 72 men and sent them out two by two, to go ahead of him to every town and place where he himself was about to go. (Verse 1)

Jesus needed helpers. He knew that his time in Galilee was coming to an end. He had travelled to many places, but there was so much work to do. Jesus chose more disciples to do his work, but why such a strange number? In those days, the Jewish people believed that there were seventy-two nations in the world. Maybe Jesus knew that one day all the nations of the world would know about him. There are Christians all over the world today and each one of us can still be a helper for Jesus. We need to keep on telling his story and keep on doing his work.

Luke has written for us how Jesus wanted his disciples to live, simply and without unnecessary possessions. All through the ages there have been men and women who have tried to live this kind of life for Jesus.

A friend in need...

Luke 10:25–37

Jesus said, 'There was once a man who was going down from Jerusalem to Jericho when robbers attacked him…' And Jesus concluded, 'In your opinion, which one of these three acted like a neighbour towards the man attacked by the robbers?' (Verses 30 and 36)

There is a famous story about a highwayman called Dick Turpin and his horse Black Bess. The story is so caught up in the notion of brave Dick and his ride through the night to avoid being captured that it is easy to forget that there were victims too.

Jesus knew that the twenty-mile journey from Jerusalem to Jericho was a lonely and dangerous one. He chose the location of his story well. He also chose the characters very well—the traveller who was foolish enough to make the journey alone, the priest who could not risk breaking the rules of the Temple by touching the injured man, and the Levite, who was too afraid to help. Then there was the Samaritan, an enemy of the injured man, but the only one who helped him. Jesus asks us to 'love your neighbour as yourself'.

Luke 9:46—10:37

Things to do

Help!

I can be a neighbour to...

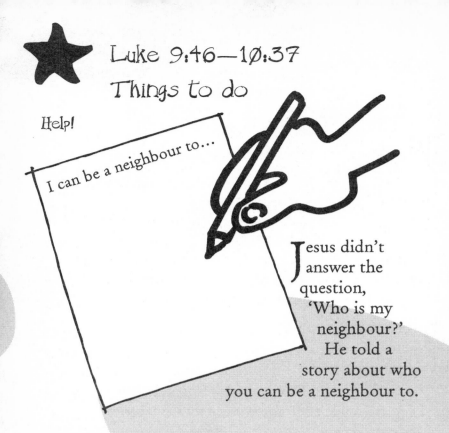

Jesus didn't answer the question, 'Who is my neighbour?' He told a story about who you can be a neighbour to.

Make a list of people you can be a neighbour to.

Toby + Trish
Rescue dog

Why is it that whenever I shout for help...

Boomerang lands on top of me!

56
Just imagine making the sandwiches at your own birthday party!

Martha and Mary

Luke 10:38–42

'Mary has chosen the right thing, and it will not be taken away from her.' (Verse 42)

Just imagine that someone you haven't seen for ages, someone that you really like, is coming to your house. You just know they will have brought you something special. You can hardly wait for them to come. Then, just after they arrive, your mum sends you to the shop. She has forgotten to buy enough milk!

Well, Jesus visited a home where he was very welcome. The two sisters, Martha and Mary, were pleased he had come. Martha wanted everything to be just right with her home, but Mary just wanted to be with Jesus. Mary had got it right! It is more important to listen to what Jesus has to say than to fuss over unnecessary things.

57

How to pray
Luke 11:1–13

Jesus said to them, 'When you pray, say this: "Father: may your holy name be honoured; may your Kingdom come."' (Verse 2)

Most of the things that you know how to do well have been taught to you by someone else—maybe by a parent, a grandparent, a teacher at school or your group of friends. The disciples had been taught many things by Jesus—how to live, how to heal, how to tell others about him. Luke tells us about the day that they asked him to teach them to pray. Jesus taught them to think of God as their Father and to call God 'Father' when they prayed. Jesus used the Aramaic word 'Abba' which literally means 'Daddy'.

The prayer Jesus taught us to say is sometimes called 'The Lord's Prayer' or 'The Family Prayer'. Why not say it out loud now!

What has Jonah got to do with it?
Luke 11:14–32

Others wanted to trap Jesus, so they asked him to perform a miracle to show that God approved of him… As the people crowded round Jesus, he went on to say, 'How evil are the people of this day! They ask for a miracle, but none will be given them except the miracle of Jonah.' (Verses 16 and 29)

People were always asking for miracles—for proof that Jesus really was the Son of God. How tired he must have been of having to keep on telling them how to recognize the truth! First of all, Luke tells us that Jesus never performed miracles just to be popular. He was always true to himself and to God. Luke then tells us how Jesus compared his situation to Jonah and to Solomon. Jonah was a prophet with a message to tell—you can read all about him in his amazing book. Solomon was a wise king whom everyone listened to.

Everyone would have known about these two famous men, but they could not see that Jesus was greater than either of them!

59

You didn't wash your hands!

Luke 11:33–53

'Make certain, then, that the light in you is not darkness. If your whole body is full of light, with no part of it in darkness, it will be bright all over, as when a lamp shines on you with its brightness.' When Jesus finished speaking, a Pharisee invited him to eat with him; so he went in and sat down to eat. (Verses 35–37)

The minute Jesus sits down, the Pharisee accuses him of not washing his hands before eating. Jesus replies, 'Now then, you Pharisees clean the outside of your cup and plate, but inside you are full of violence and evil.'

'Wash your hands before dinner!' We know that this is a good thing to do. Washing makes sure that germs are cleansed away before we touch our food. But Jesus knew that it was no good being clean on the outside if on the inside we were full of wrong thoughts and ideas. 'Make sure that you don't have darkness inside,' he says.

Can you think of people like that? But take care you don't become like them!

Undercover agents!

Luke 12:1–12

'Be on guard against the yeast of the Pharisees—I mean their hypocrisy. Whatever is covered up will be uncovered, and every secret will be made known.' (Verses 1 and 2)

Sometimes you might get out of bed in a really bad mood. You may not know why, but it just won't go away! Everyone you meet becomes affected by your bad mood, until they are all as grumpy as you. This is a very strange thing and it is difficult to understand how it happens.

Jesus told us that it is like having yeast inside us—the living ingredient added to the dough to make bread light and fluffy. The yeast cannot be seen, but it works very well by multiplying itself inside the dough. Yeast is a good thing to have, but moods and bad secrets and bad thoughts about others tend to grow in much the same way. None of these things is good to have!

Luke 10:38—12:12

Things to do

Mobile phone

Make yourself a 'mobile phone' out of a piece of cardboard. Instead of numbers on the buttons, write OUR * FATHER to remind you that you can speak to God any time of the day or night.

Toby + Trish Dial-a-problem

A recorded voice said they're closed *but* they'll send one round when they open... whenever that might *be*

It's who you are, not what you've got, that counts!

Luke 12:13–34

I can't count... so where does that leave me?

'There was once a rich man who had land which bore good crops. He began to think to himself, "...Lucky man! You have all the good things you need for many years..." But God said to him, "You fool!"' (Verses 16–17 and 19–20)

Would you like to have the very latest designer trainers, the latest video game, and holidays every year in Florida? Do you think that you would be the happiest person you know? Would all your friends have the same as you, or would they begin to feel left out? Having nice things is all right as long as having them doesn't become too important.

A man called Howard Hughes was very rich. He bought bigger and bigger houses and more and more things to put in them. He began to mistrust his friends and to think that they might steal his fine things. He shut himself away from everyone and became a very lonely old man. Jesus tells us that possessions are not important—it's the sort of people we are that really counts.

62

Making good use of time
Luke 12:35-48

'Be ready for what ever comes, dressed for action and with your lamps lit, like servants who are waiting for their master to come back from a wedding feast... because the Son of Man will come at an hour when you are not expecting him.' (Verses 35, 36 and 40)

Sometimes we hear people say, 'It's a gift from God' when someone is really good at something. It may be singing or painting or sports or some other outstanding achievement. We all have gifts from God—things that we are good at doing—but some people waste their gifts. They are too lazy to use them well.

Jesus promised that he would return one day. No one knows when that will be. What a terrible thing it would be if Jesus came and found that the gifts God has given us had been wasted and not used! Find out what your gifts are. It may be being a good friend, a listener, an animal lover, or a gardener. Use those gifts well!

Being a good Christian
Luke 12:49–53

'I came to set the earth on fire, and how I wish it were already kindled!' (Verse 49)

Our new Sunday school teacher is called Miss Burns

Have you ever watched a forest fire on the television? It's a frightening thing to see. It burns everything in its path, the tallest tree and the youngest green shoot on the forest floor. Being a Christian is a bit like being a forest fire. Once it is started, it's impossible to put it out.

Jesus warns us about Christians who start well but allow others to change what they believe and how they live. They are not forest fires but just damp, smouldering smoke! If we are to follow Jesus, nothing must stand in the way.

Dear Jesus, you have set us a challenge. Help us to be 'on fire' for you. Amen

Sort out your quarrels!

Luke 12:54–59

'You can look at the earth and the sky and predict the weather; why, then, don't you know the meaning of the present time? Why do you not judge for yourselves the right thing to do?' (Verses 56 and 57))

'Red sky in the morning, shepherds' warning; red sky at night, shepherds' delight!' This old saying is supposed to predict the weather for the day. The people who lived in Galilee would have had similar sayings. To understand the weather was important to them. The right time to sow seeds, the right time to start a long journey on foot—so many things depended on the weather.

Jesus knew all this, but he also knew that the people had not read the signs about his coming to earth. They had ignored the signs about the most important things. He wanted them to sort out their quarrels with each other, to put their affairs in order and to be at peace with God.

Cut down the fig tree!
Luke 13:1–9

There was once a man who had a fig tree growing in his vineyard. He went looking for figs on it but found none. So he said to his gardener, 'Cut it down!' But the gardener answered, 'Leave it alone, sir, just one more year.' *(Verses 6–8)*

Some day you may have a garden of your own. You will dig the soil, add fertilizer and sow some seeds. You may go to the garden centre and choose some plants you have always wanted. The garden is planted and after all the hard work you can sit back and wait for things to grow. You will expect lots of flowers and lush, green growth. But something goes wrong. An expensive plant looks very sick—no flowers, and yellow leaves. What should you do? Do you pull it out or feed it and wait another year?

Jesus knew that we can be like a garden. He can plant his ideas for us to follow, but if we don't look after them properly they will wither away, just like a plant. To follow Jesus takes constant care!

Luke 12:13—13:9

Things to do

Using up the soil

Circle the 'good fruit' that can come out of your life.

Toby + Trish — Using the soil

Would he notice if I pinched the plant pot and put pansies in it?

Rules to be broken

Luke 13:10–17

The official of the synagogue was angry that Jesus had healed on the Sabbath, so he spoke up and said to the people, 'There are six days in which we should work; so come during those days and be healed, but not on the Sabbath!' (Verse 14)

Have you ever heard the expression, 'It's more than my job's worth'? There are many people who will not put themselves out in any way to help others. They will only do the absolute minimum, and sometimes they may seem to be deliberately difficult. Jesus knew lots of people like that! They were so intent on obeying the religious laws that they had forgotten how to be kind to one another.

The synagogue leader was one of these people. He was really angry that Jesus had healed a woman on the Sabbath day—a day when no work was to be done. Jesus was angry with him for thinking that anyone should suffer a day longer than was necessary, and the crowd agreed with him. Jesus had made friends and enemies that day.

67

More parables
Luke 13:18–30

Jesus asked, 'What is the Kingdom of God like? What shall I compare it with?' (Verse 18)

Have you ever grown mustard and cress seeds on blotting paper or cottonwool? The seeds are very small, like black dust, but if they are watered and kept warm they will soon grow into plants that can be picked and used for cooking.

Jesus knew about seeds. Maybe he had grown some himself at home in Nazareth! He knew that from something small something big could grow. He must have watched Mary, his mother, make bread countless times. He had watched the yeast work on the dough. Yet the yeast grains are so small that they cannot be seen by the human eye.

The Kingdom of God can grow just like a seed or like yeast. If it is given the right conditions, it will soon be very big indeed. Are you willing to help the Kingdom of God grow?

68

Trust and obey
For there's no other way
To be happy in Jesus
But to trust and obey

Jerusalem calls
Luke 13:31-35

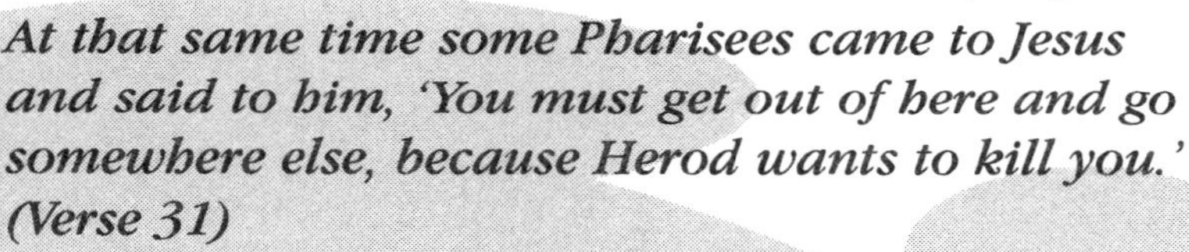

At that same time some Pharisees came to Jesus and said to him, 'You must get out of here and go somewhere else, because Herod wants to kill you.' (Verse 31)

Even the Pharisees liked Jesus more than they liked Herod! The Pharisees, who were so against Jesus' teaching, came to try to warn him that Herod wanted him dead. Jesus calls Herod 'a fox', a name given to a sly person.

But even Herod could not decide when Jesus would stop teaching about God and begin the journey to Jerusalem—where his death would await him. This was something only God could decide. Jesus trusted his heavenly Father so much that he relied on him every step of the way. Do you trust God that much?

Dinner with a Pharisee
Luke 14:1–24

Jesus went to eat a meal at the home of one of the leading Pharisees… A man whose legs and arms were swollen came to Jesus… Jesus healed him and sent him away… Jesus noticed how some of the guests were choosing the best places, so he told this parable to all of them: 'When someone invites you to a wedding feast, do not sit down in the best place…' (Verses 1–2, 4 and 7–8)

Best place to sit is near the kitchen door

Luke has written about seven different times when Jesus healed on the Sabbath. This time it is at the home of one of the Pharisees. Do you think the Pharisee made sure there was a sick person there to see what Jesus would do?

Jesus noticed that the guests at the meal were filling all the good seats first and he used this incident to teach about our feelings of self-importance. Do you know anyone who always pushes to the front of the dinner queue or takes the best cricket bat at games time? Do you like them very much?

Give up everything you have!

Luke 14:25-35

I don't want to give up reading my Bible, though!

Once when large crowds of people were going along with Jesus, he turned and said to them, 'Those who come to me cannot be my disciples unless they love me more than they love father and mother, wife and children, brothers and sisters, and themselves as well.' (Verses 25 and 26)

A martyr is someone who believes that to love Jesus is more important than anything else in the whole world—so important that they are willing to die rather than say anything against Jesus. There have been many thousands of people who have died for their faith in Jesus. Some of them are remembered throughout the year on special days, such as Paul and Peter. Can you find out some things about them?

If we really believe in Jesus, we should be prepared to give up everything to do the right thing for him. Are we ready to love him that much?

Luke 13:10—14:35

Things to do

Every step of the way

Around the footprint, write all the things we can trust Jesus for.

Toby + Trish Painful steps

You can't hear other people puffing and panting until you get in front of them

Things that are lost
Luke 15:1–32

'In the same way, I tell you, the angels of God rejoice over one sinner who repents.' (Verse 10)

Have you ever lost something valuable to you? Did you find it? Jesus told three stories about losing things and finding them again.

Jesus would have watched shepherds at work—he knew how important every single sheep was. He knew that a shepherd would search for the one sheep that was lost, like in the first story. Jesus understood the happiness at finding it. In the second story, the woman who found her lost coin was also very happy when it was found. But, in the third story, how much happier was the father when his son who had been lost came home again!

Jesus tells us that God is very happy every time someone returns to loving him. He forgives all that they have done wrong and welcomes them back.

72

Well, I'm certainly looking after my money. I can't get it out of my piggy bank!

God and money!
Luke 16:1–18

'No servant can be the slave of two masters; such a servant will hate one and love the other... You cannot serve both God and money.' (Verse 13)

'Save the pennies and the pounds will look after themselves!' is a very old proverb. It has a lot of truth in it. Every day on the television we see adverts tempting us to buy lots of things—things that many of us don't really need. Have you ever hankered after the latest Christmas present fad? If you were given it, do you think that the money was wisely spent?

Jesus teaches us that looking after money is important, but serving God is even more important! Jesus knows that someone who is able to 'look after the pennies' is most likely be a careful person, thinking ahead and planning well. How much better that sort of person might be in serving God, in thinking and planning ahead.

Father God, please help me to make you the most important thing in my life. Amen

Punishment

Luke 16:19–31

But Abraham said, 'Remember, my son, that in your lifetime you were given all the good things, while Lazarus got all the bad things. But now he is enjoying himself here, while you are in pain.' (Verse 25)

Luke is the only Gospel writer to give us this story. Jesus warns the Pharisees and the crowd that how they live their life on earth really matters. Jesus has given us a very clear picture of both heaven and hell! He tells us about the poor man, Lazarus, who suffered greatly while he was alive, and the rich man who did nothing to help him. After death, things are reversed. It is the rich man who suffers because he did not use the opportunities that God gave him to help other people.

Here is a very old prayer that the rich man should have learnt.

Dear Lord, three things I pray: to know you more clearly, to love you more dearly, to follow you more nearly, day by day. Amen

There's lots of sin about!

Luke 17:1–10

I had a bite of Kylie's chocolate bar before she told me she hadn't paid for it!

Jesus said to his disciples, 'Things that make people fall into sin are bound to happen, but how terrible for the one who makes them happen! It would be better for him if a large millstone were tied round his neck and he were thrown into the sea than for him to cause one of these little ones to sin.' (Verses 1 and 2)

The days were running out. Jesus was getting nearer and nearer to Jerusalem, but there was still so much to teach people! He wanted people to be sure of how to live and of their place in heaven. Jesus knows that people are tempted to do wrong by all sorts of things, but how much worse it is when someone else is persuaded to join in!

Do you know anyone in school who sometimes misses a lesson? Do they try to get you to join them? What do you do? Jesus wants us to think for ourselves, to make up our own minds and, most of all, to try not to get other people into trouble.

Thank you!
Luke 17:11–19

I didn't say thank you to the doctor for giving me that injection

As Jesus made his way to Jerusalem, he went into a village when he was met by ten men suffering from a dreaded skin disease. They stood at a distance and shouted, 'Jesus! Master! Take pity on us!' (Verses 11–13)

Imagine waking up one morning to find your whole body covered in spots. You are itchy and hot and not feeling at all well. A visit to the doctor is arranged and then you find out that you have a new disease. No one has ever seen it before. There is no cure! The doctor tells you that you will have to live in a sealed room. No one can come in and your food must be passed through a special hatch. How would you be feeling?

Leprosy was a bit like that. It was so awful that no one would come near for fear of catching it. Jesus did something no one else would do—he helped the lepers. Do you think they all should have said, 'Thank you'? Luke tells us that only one did this. He was a stranger, a man from Samaria.

Luke 15:1—17:19

Things to do

One in ten

Find ten counters, Smarties or mints, with one a different colour from the rest. Now see if you can arrange them in straight lines with the one (the man who said 'thank you') in the middle. The pattern must be the same whichever way you look at it. (Answer on page 128.)

Why is it that if you hurt just one finger, it gets in the way of everything?

76

Like a flash of lightning!

Luke 17:20–37

Some Pharisees asked Jesus when the Kingdom of God would come. His answer was, 'The Kingdom of God does not come in such a way as to be seen… As the lightning flashes across the sky and lights it up from one side to the other, so will the Son of Man be in his day.' (Verses 20 and 24)

Have you ever been caught suddenly in a storm? The sky changes, the clouds begin to gather and everything seems very dark. And then suddenly the whole sky is lit for a few seconds with a flash of lightning! It can be very beautiful as well as very frightening and even dangerous.

Jesus was coming closer and closer to Jerusalem. He had spent three years travelling and teaching. The Pharisees were always trying to trick him into saying something against the religious laws. The disciples still didn't understand who he was. How Jesus must have despaired! Yet again, he tried to explain that he would soon be gone from them, but one day he would come again—suddenly, like a flash of lightning.

It will be a beautiful and dangerous time.

77

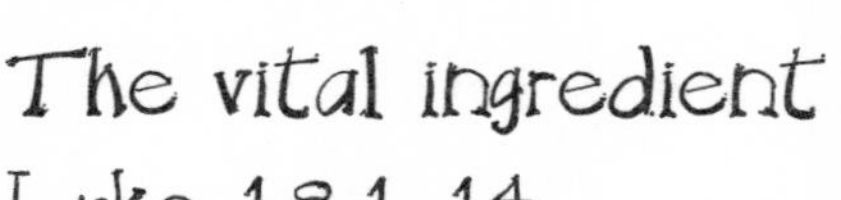

The vital ingredient
Luke 18:1–14

Jesus also told this parable to people who were sure of their own goodness and despised everybody else. 'Once there were two men who went up to the Temple to pray...' (Verses 9 and 10)

When your birthday comes, you may be lucky enough to have a party. Imagine that the day has come and your friends are all sitting at the table to eat and the birthday cake is cut. Then, horror of horrors, it tastes awful. No one remembered to add the sugar! A vital ingredient was missing.

The Pharisee in Jesus' story is like that cake. He only went to the Temple to pray because it made him look good. The vital ingredient was missing. He had no compassion or sense of humility. Jesus knows that lots of people will try to follow him, but without the vital ingredient of loving each other it will all be worthless.

Children are very welcome

Luke 18:15–17

'Remember this! Whoever does not receive the Kingdom of God like a child will never enter it.' (Verse 17)

'Don't bother Jesus. He's too tired!' the disciples say. Jesus was tired. He had travelled a long way. Jerusalem was near, and all that waited for him there. The disciples and the women in the travelling group had looked after him—and watched him change—in the past few days. They were worried about him, so they tried to stop the children from bothering him. But Jesus would have none of it and he said, 'Let the children come to me and do not stop them, for the Kingdom of God belongs to these.'

Thank you, Lord Jesus, that even the smallest child is important to you. Amen

79

A camel and a needle!

Luke 18:18-30

'It is much harder for a rich person to enter the Kingdom of God than for a camel to go through the eye of a needle.' (Verse 25)

A magician once performed a wonderful trick. A woman was locked inside a steel box with many padlocks and chains, and the key was given to a member of the audience to hold. With a wave of the magician's wand and a few strange words, the woman appeared at the back of the stage. How was it done? Had the audience been tricked? Is there anything that is really impossible?

Jesus uses this amusing picture of the camel and the eye of the needle to bring home a very important truth. It is impossible to follow God if we hang on to our own selfishness as well.

Jesus explains again
Luke 18:31–34

"The news never makes sense to me—even though it's in English!"

Jesus took the twelve disciples aside and said to them, 'Listen! We are going to Jerusalem where everything the prophets wrote about the Son of Man will come true.' ... But the disciples did not understand any of these things; the meaning of the words was hidden from them, and they did not know what Jesus was talking about. (Verses 31 and 34)

Sometimes a film comes on the television that is in another language. The film-makers have made sure that a subtitle line is running along the bottom of the screen so that the viewers can read the words for themselves. But if the viewers' attention wanders, it is easy for the meaning of the film to be lost.

Jesus wanted so much for his disciples to understand the meaning of his life—why he was to die and that he would rise again from the dead. He had tried many times to explain it to them, and here he is, trying once again.

But his words just didn't make sense to them.

Luke 17:20—18:34

Things to do

It's camel time!

The thing you love most is the thing you spend longest thinking about. Trace the camel and the needle on to card and cut them out. Push the camel through the eye of the needle to remind you not to think too much about things you own—or want to own.

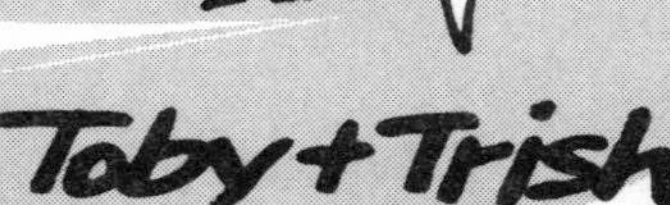

Toby + Trish Trish on camel

It travels a long way in the desert because it stores fat in its hump and water in its stomach. With a few potatoes and some teabags we could have chips and a cup of tea...

The man who wouldn't give up

Luke 18:35-43

As Jesus was coming near Jericho, there was a blind man sitting by the road, begging... He cried out, 'Jesus! Son of David! Take pity on me!' (Verses 35 and 38)

There is a story about a young boy who lived in Holland, who put his finger into a hole in one of the flood barriers to stop it leaking. The boy would not give up—he stayed there until help came, and saved his village from terrible flooding.

The blind man knew that Jesus was near. Jesus was his last hope of ever seeing again. He just would not give up! Others tried to stop him from shouting, but Jesus heard and stopped what he was doing to heal the man.

Lord Jesus, please help me to understand that knowing all about you is so important that I mustn't stop until I have found out as much as I can. Amen

Jesus and Zacchaeus

Luke 19:1-10

Jesus went on into Jericho and was passing though… Zacchaeus ran ahead of the crowd and climbed a sycomore tree to see Jesus… When Jesus came to that place, he looked up and said to Zacchaeus, 'Hurry down, Zacchaeus, because I must stay in your house today.' (Verses 1, 4 and 5)

Poor old Zacchaeus! No one liked him. He had no friends in Jericho. He had cheated so many people out of their money. He wasn't even a fine-looking fellow. (Luke tells us he was 'a little man'.) Maybe Zacchaeus was fed up with his life. Being rich wasn't much fun when there were no friends to impress! He had heard about Jesus—this man who spoke to anyone, even tax collectors! Jesus was his last chance. Here was someone who would bother with him!

What a comical sight Zaccaeus must have made, scurrying up a tree to get a good view. And how surprised he must have been when Jesus stopped and called him down. Zacchaeus was right, Jesus did have time for him. He even went to his house.

Jesus has time for everyone.

83

Golden coins

Luke 19:11-27

'I tell you,' the king replied, 'that to all those who have something, even more will be given; but those who have nothing, even the little that they have will be taken away from them.' (Verse 26)

During a great snooker tournament, one of the players was interviewed at the practice table. He was asked, 'Why is it, when you are ranked among the top ten players in the world, that you still practise for many hours on the day of the match?' He answered, 'If I don't practise every day, my gift may be taken away from me!'

The king in the story tested his servants to see which of them would use their gifts to look after his money. Two of them did well, but the third did not do anything and everything was taken away from him.

The judgment might seem harsh, but it is true. If we don't use our gifts, we may lose them. God wants us to use our gifts and serve him well.

Jesus enters Jerusalem

Luke 19:28-40

When Jesus came near Jerusalem, at the place where the road went down the Mount of Olives, the large crowd of his disciples began to thank God and praise him in loud voices for all the great things that they had seen. (Verse 37)

When someone important is coming to visit a town, special arrangements will be made to greet them. The mayor will be there wearing his golden chain. People will line up to shake hands and a red carpet will be laid on the floor for them to walk on.

The journey from Jericho to Jerusalem was seventeen miles. It had been a difficult journey with lots of interruptions. When Jesus arrived in Jerusalem, he came as someone important—he arrived as a king. There wasn't a red carpet but the floor was covered with palm branches, and the crowds shouted their greetings and lined the streets to shake his hand!

Tears and anger

Luke 19:41-48

Jesus came closer to the city, and when he saw it, he wept over it. (Verse 41)

Jesus had been to Jerusalem many times. He knew it well and loved going there. As he travelled down the Mount of Olives, he was high above the city and could see all of it spread below. A moment of great sadness came over him, because he knew that this beautiful place would one day be in ruins.

Luke tells us that the first place Jesus went to in Jerusalem was the Temple. He went there to teach, but he found the courtyard full of market stalls and money lenders. Do you think Jesus could be really angry? Well, on this day he was! He turned the tables over and made the stallholders leave. The temple leaders were not pleased. Jesus had made more enemies.

Luke 18:35—19:48
Things to do

What a difference!

Zacchaeus went up a tree miserable and came down happy! See if you can draw his face looking sad and then turn it the other way up and make him smile. He's found his greatest friend—Jesus!

Toby + Trish Whoops!

There's a dozen ways up, but only one way down— and I've lost it!

86
You haven't answered my question...
Well, er, before I do, er, let me just say...

Teaching in the temple
Luke 20:1-18

Jesus looked at them and asked, 'What, then, does this scripture mean? "The stone which the builders rejected as worthless turned out to be the most important of all."' (Verse 17)

When an election is due, the politicians try to outdo one another with their questions and their answers. But sometimes they get really flustered if a question is asked that they don't want to answer. Sometimes the person doing the interview deliberately tries to trick them into saying something they will regret.

The religious leaders in the Temple tried to do this to Jesus. They kept asking difficult questions to trick Jesus into saying something against them. His answer is clever, but it lets the leaders know that Jesus believes himself to be the Son of God.

Even more questions!

Luke 20:19-47

Master, we know you are wise, but can you just remind us why it is that...

The teachers of the Law and the chief priests tried to arrest Jesus on the spot… but they were afraid of the people. So they looked for an opportunity. They bribed some men to pretend they were sincere, and they sent them to trap Jesus with questions, so that they could hand him over to the authority and power of the Roman Governor. (Verses 19 and 20)

A spy is someone who pretends to be on your side, a friend who is really an enemy. They listen and watch all that you do, and then go and tell everything they know to someone who will pay them money for the information.

The religious leaders sent spies to watch Jesus. The questions kept on coming. Questions about taxes to be paid to the hated Romans, questions about death and marriage, questions about God's promised king. Jesus answered them all and still they did not manage to trick him!

His enemies became even more angry.

Everything she had!

Luke 21:1–4

Jesus looked round and saw rich people dropping their gifts in the temple treasury, and he also saw a very poor widow dropping in two little copper coins. (Verses 1 and 2)

Imagine sitting for hours turning an old eggbox into a gift for someone special. You enjoy painting it, putting the glitter on and lining the inside with tissue paper so that it will hold a few sweets. Imagine the delight on the face of that special person as you give your precious gift! It cost only a few pennies, but it was all you had and you gave time to make someone smile.

Jesus watched the poor widow put her money into the temple money box, and he knew that she had given everything she had. He also watched the rich people select their coins and put some back in their pockets! God wants us to give everything we have to him and keep nothing back.

Beautiful things can be destroyed

Luke 21:5–28

'When you see Jerusalem surrounded by armies, then you will know that it will soon be destroyed.' (Verse 20)

Have you ever spent a summer's day on a sandy beach? Imagine getting together with your friends to spend the whole morning building a sand city. Every house and detail is carefully made and when it is finished it all looks very beautiful in the sunshine. The next morning when you get up, eager to finish your work, you find that the tide has come in during the night and the sand city lies in ruins. All of its beauty has gone.

Jesus tried to warn his disciples that one day the beautiful city of Jerusalem would also lie in ruins. His warning came true about forty years later.

90

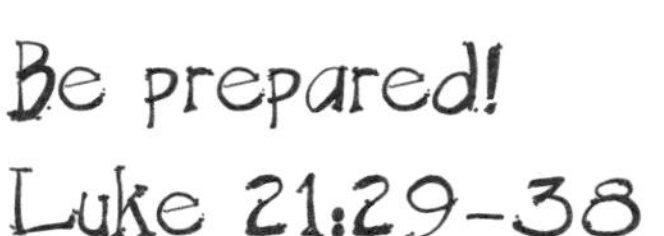

Be prepared! Luke 21:29–38

'Be on your guard! … Be on the alert and pray always that you will have the strength to go safely through all those things that will happen and to stand before the Son of Man.' (Verses 34 and 36)

The Girl Guides and the Boy Scouts have a motto: 'Be Prepared'. When Lord Baden-Powell started the first Scout group, he taught the boys all sorts of tips that would be useful in an emergency. The Scouts learnt how to light a fire with one match, how to build a shelter, how to signal to each other if they got lost. Lord Baden-Powell knew that you could never tell what is going to happen in the future, so it's much better to be ready to deal with it whatever it is!

Jesus tried to warn his disciples to be alert, to be prepared for whatever the future would bring.

Luke 20:1—21:38

Things to do

Switched on

Motorists have rear-view mirrors... Birds stop every second when they're eating to look around...

Practise looking round and listening to what is going on around you all day.

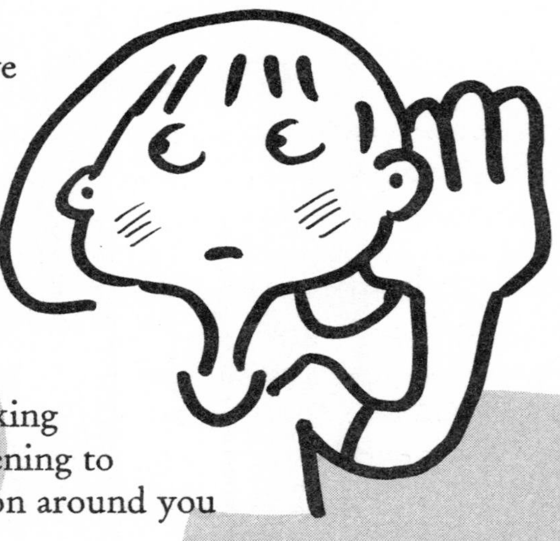

Toby + Trish
Switched off

Why is it that when you switch on the telly you switch off your brain?

The part that Judas played Luke 22:1-6

So Judas went off and spoke with the chief priests and the officers of the temple guard about how he could betray Jesus to them. (Verse 4)

How would you describe a king? Maybe you would expect him to wear expensive clothes and a golden crown. Perhaps he would live in a huge palace surrounded by servants who fetched and carried for him. When the king travelled, he would have a huge, comfortable car. Noise and dust would never enter it! Would you expect him to talk to any person who called out from a crowd, to stop and touch those who were poor, unwell or beggars? Would you expect him to let other people insult him and try to trick him, or not even to have a house of his own?

Poor Judas. He couldn't understand this king. To him, Jesus was a big disappointment! Judas decided to help the religious leaders capture Jesus. He wasn't the sort of king that Judas wanted.

The Lord's Supper

Luke 22:7–23

The disciples went off and found everything just as Jesus had told them, and they prepared the Passover meal. When the hour came, Jesus took his place at the table with the apostles. (Verses 13 and 14)

Everyone loves a special party. It's a time to meet with friends, a time to wear your best clothes and eat good food. Every year, Buckingham Palace prepares for a special party, a garden party, where people from all over the country are invited to tea with the Queen. The preparations are very careful. The lawn is cut, the flowers grown, the tables and chairs set out in rows and the food is carried into huge, striped tents. It is an honour to be invited.

But even this meal is not as important as the one Jesus prepared for at Passover in Jerusalem. During the meal, Jesus gave instructions for the apostles to continue to eat bread and wine together after he was gone. We still remember him in this way in our churches today.

Everything was just right. It really was an honour to be invited. But one man already knew that he would let Jesus down.

93

Another quarrel

Luke 22:24–38

Well, there's never any argument about who's the least in this family!

An argument broke out among the disciples as to which one of them should be thought of as the greatest. Jesus said to them, '... Who is greater, the one who sits down to eat or the one who serves him? The one who sits down, of course. But I am among you as one who serves.' (Verses 24, 25 and 27)

There's an old saying, 'Manners maketh man'. It means that manners are very important. Many huge books have been written about manners—the right things to do in all sorts of situations.

The religious leaders in Jesus' day had all sorts of rules about manners to do with eating. They even had a rule for where people should sit at the table. Jesus had prepared this last meal with his disciples, but they were only concerned about who sat nearest to him—the guest of honour. The seats nearest were thought to be more important than those further away.

Even now, at this last, important meal together, the disciples quarrel over stupid, unimportant things.

Betrayed in a garden

Luke 22:39-53

Jesus left the city and went, as he usually did, to the Mount of Olives; and his disciples went with him... Judas came up to Jesus to kiss him. But Jesus said, 'Judas, is it with a kiss that you betray the Son of Man?' (Verses 39, 47 and 48)

If you visit a garden centre, you may see some concrete plaques. Written on them it will say, 'You are nearer to God in a garden than anywhere else on earth'. How true this was for the disciples the night of the Passover supper!

When the meal was over, Jesus led them to the garden on the Mount of Olives where he liked to go and pray. He prayed so hard that sweat like drops of blood fell from his forehead to the ground. It was here that Judas brought the crowd and the priests to arrest Jesus. Judas really didn't know that night how close he was to God in that garden.

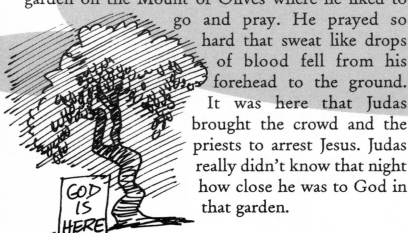

'I don't know him!'

Luke 22:54-62

The Lord turned round and looked straight at Peter, and Peter remembered that the Lord had said to him, 'Before the cock crows tonight, you will say three times that you do not know me.' Peter went out and wept bitterly. (Verses 61 and 62)

When the Fire Brigade attend a suspicious fire, one of the firemen is given the job of looking around the crowd to see if anyone is acting strangely. It's a strange fact that someone who starts a fire almost always hangs around on the edge of the crowd to see the result.

Peter hadn't started the chain of events, but he wanted to see what was going to happen to Jesus. So he hung around. More than anything, he was afraid of being seen and arrested as well. Jesus had already told Peter that he would say three times that he didn't know him before the cock crowed that night. And, just as Jesus had said, Peter was asked three times if he knew Jesus. Three times he said 'no'! Then the cock crowed.

Luke 22:1–62

Things to do

In memory of me

Some people tie a knot in their hankies to remind them of something.

Tie a knot in your hanky to remind you to say, 'Thank you, Lord Jesus, for loving me enough to die for me.'

Toby + Trish Bad memory

I just can't remember these words for the test...
I'm not surprised. You've forgotten I'm your dog and it's tea-time!

Beaten and tried
Luke 22:63–71

The men who were guarding Jesus mocked him and beat him… When day came, the elders, the chief priests, and the teachers of the Law met together, and Jesus was brought before the Council. (Verses 63 and 66)

A law court is usually a quiet, well ordered place. Everything is done calmly and without any rush. The prisoners are well treated and allowed to give their side of the story. When all of the evidence is heard, the jury will decide the sentence.

It wasn't at all like this for Jesus. It was a hurried, dirty affair. The judges had already decided he was guilty. The Council met in the dark of the night—they wanted to be done with Jesus once and for all! They tried once more to trick him into saying things that would make their task seem legal. But Jesus would not be tricked. He would not help them. He remained calm and with great dignity throughout it all.

97

Where are all Jesus' friends and the people he healed...?

Pilate and Herod

Luke 23:1–25

The whole group rose up and took Jesus before Pilate... Pilate asked him, 'Are you the king of the Jews?' 'So you say,' answered Jesus. Then Pilate said to the chief priests and the crowds, 'I find no reason to condemn this man.' (Verses 1, 3 and 4)

Pontius Pilate was Governor of Judea. He worked for the Romans. He was known to be a cruel man.

Pilate had a problem. He did not want to say that Jesus had to die, so he decided to send him to Herod (who was in Jerusalem at the time) for him to make the decision. Herod had waited a long time to meet Jesus. He wanted him to perform some miracles for him. But Jesus refused even to speak to Herod, so he was sent back to Pilate.

Pilate was not at all pleased. He decided to let the crowd choose between Jesus and Barabbas—who was a dangerous criminal—to see who should be set free. The crowds shouted for Barabbas to be released. Pilate had no choice. Jesus was to die.

A place called 'The Skull'

Luke 23:26–43

Two other men, both of them criminals, were also led out to be put to death with Jesus. When they came to the place called 'The Skull', they crucified Jesus there... Jesus said, 'Forgive them, Father! They don't know what they are doing.' (Verses 32–34)

Imagine being blamed for something you didn't do. No matter how hard you try to explain, no one will listen. How would you feel? Hurt, upset, let down?

Jesus had done nothing wrong. He was an innocent man. His death was not fair. The religious leaders had plotted against him. There was nothing he could say or do that would have stopped those awful things from happening.

Lord Jesus, thank you that you went willingly to the place called 'The Skull'. Thank you for taking the blame for all the things that I have ever done wrong. Amen

Darkness at midday

Luke 23:44-56

Jesus cried out in a loud voice, 'Father! In your hands I place my spirit!' He said this and died. (Verse 46)

Many years before Jesus' death, King Solomon had built his Temple. It was flooded with a great light—a sign to the people that God was there. The priests had placed curtains around the most holy part of the Temple to try to keep God away from the people. At the moment when Jesus died, Luke tells us that the sun stopped shining and darkness covered the whole country. At that moment, the temple curtain was torn into two and, as daylight returned, light flooded once again into the Temple. Jesus had opened the way for everyone to reach God.

After his death, Jesus was buried according to the custom of the day. A great sadness came over the disciples and the women of the group. But the next day was the Sabbath. A day of resting… and waiting…

He is not here
Luke 24:1- 12

Very early on Sunday morning the women went to the tomb, carrying the spices they had prepared. They found the stone rolled away from the entrance to the tomb... but they did not find the body of the Lord Jesus. (Verses 1–3)

When people are really sad, they tend to be very quiet and thoughtful. All their movements show how sad they are. Can you imagine the women as they walked to the tomb early on the Sunday morning? Can you imagine how puzzled they must have been when they found that the huge stone had been moved away? They could hardly believe their eyes!

And then they remembered! Jesus had told them all this would happen. How could they have doubted him? The women just *had* to share the news with the others. How differently they left that tomb! No longer sadly and slowly, but quickly and full of joy!

Luke 22:63—24:12

Things to do

Pop-up Easter card

Let's celebrate this happy day with a card like a shining light!

Fold an A4 sheet of paper in half and in half again. Draw an Easter picture on the front of the card. Colour the inside in yellow and write the words JESUS IS ALIVE along the bottom. Take a second A4 sheet and cut off a 60mm strip. Write the word ALLELUIA in bold letters across the strip and decorate it in bright colours. Concertina the strip by folding it backwards and forwards. The folds should each be approximately 10mm wide. Tape or glue the folded strip to the inside of the card as shown, with the word ALLELUIA uppermost.

JESUS IS ALIVE!

Toby + Trish
Not in the graveyard
I love reading the names on old gravestones
But there's one name you won't find—Jesus. He's alive for ever. Hurray!

A stranger on the road
Luke 24:13–32

On that same day two of Jesus' followers were going to a village named Emmaus… and they were talking to each other about all the things that had happened. As they talked and discussed, Jesus himself drew near and walked along with them. (Verses 13–15)

Sometimes we need to talk something over with a friend—something so important that we just need to get away from anyone else. Two of Jesus' friends felt just like that.

Cleopas and his friend were so engrossed in their conversation that when a man joined them they didn't bother to look too closely at him. They even began to tell this person about all the things that had happened in Jerusalem. Maybe the stranger could help them sort out the things they didn't understand! The stranger didn't disappoint them. He told them so many things about Jesus that they even invited him to stay with them. It was then that they realized who he was.

Can you imagine how they felt? Now they really believed that Jesus was alive again.

It's all here
and
it's true!

Jesus keeps his promise
Luke 24:33–49

They got up at once and went back to Jerusalem, where they found the eleven disciples gathered together with the others and saying, 'The Lord is risen indeed! He has appeared to Simon!' ... Suddenly, the Lord himself stood among them and said to them, 'Peace be with you.' (Verses 33, 34 and 36)

Cleopas and his friend hurried back to Jerusalem. They couldn't wait to share the good news with the others. Jesus was alive! They had seen him! And then they discovered that Peter had seen him, too!

Suddenly, he was there, in the room with them! Even now, some of them were afraid. They could not understand. It was all too good to be true. Jesus knew that they thought he was a ghost, so he asked for something to eat. And then Jesus reminded them of the scriptures that they knew so well—the scriptures that had always pointed to him.

What to do now
Luke 24:5Ø-53

Then Jesus led the disciples out of the city as far as Bethany, where he raised his hands and blessed them. As he was blessing them, he departed from them and was taken up into heaven.
(Verses 50 and 51)

Jesus kept all of his promises. He met with his disciples again to comfort them and to show them the work they had to do. Can you imagine how they were feeling? Their beloved teacher, the man they had watched die, had come back to them.

This was not an end, it was a beginning. It was the start of the greatest adventure of all time. As Jesus went into heaven to be with God, his disciples began the work of telling others about him.

And that's how Luke came to write his amazing book.

We're off to read more amazing books in the Bible. See you soon!

Lord, please help me to be ready to let the adventure go on through me. Amen

Answer to puzzle on page 94